The Hidden Bruise

Bill Bailey

Library of Congress Cataloging-in-Publication Data

This Is My New Foundation

Published by Rapier Publishing

ISBN: 979-8-9998803-1-4

Printed in the United States of America

First Edition, 2025

Legal Disclaimer for the Book

Disclaimer

The views, thoughts, and opinions in this memoir are solely those of the author and do not reflect the official policy of Rapier Solutions, its clients, affiliates, or partners. Based on personal experience, it avoids disclosing confidential or proprietary information.

Disclaimer

This nonfiction work draws from the author's memories and personal experiences. While events are accurately portrayed as remembered, some details, such as names and locations, have been altered or omitted for privacy reasons.

The opinions and perspectives shared are the author's own. Dialogue and scenes are reconstructed from memory, and personal perception informs the account.

Any resemblance to real people is coincidental or done with permission. The author and publisher are not responsible for interpretations by readers; inclusion of individuals or incidents does not imply misconduct unless clearly stated and supported.

This book explores trauma, family dynamics, emotional suppression, generational pain, and realities in Black communities. While based on lived experience and cultural stories, *The Hidden Bruise* does not diagnose, treat, or replace professional mental health care.

Some stories in this book may evoke strong emotions. Readers are encouraged to pause, reflect, and seek support—whether from a friend, faith leader, therapist, or community—if needed. Healing is not a linear process, and no single story can speak for all.

This book does not aim to assign blame, but rather to offer language, space, and compassion for often-unspoken truths. Every family is different. Every bruise is personal. This book honors both the pain and the people behind it.

The Hidden Bruise

A deeply personal, sociocultural, and intergenerational exploration of trauma, particularly within families and communities. It traces how pain is passed down, normalized, spiritualized, and often silenced—and how healing begins by naming what was never allowed to be said.

About the Author

Bill Bailey is a writer, cultural storyteller, and advocate for intergenerational healing. Drawing from lived experience, collective memory, and an unwavering commitment to honesty, Bailey's work uncovers the unspoken wounds present within families and communities, especially those shaped by race, religion, and history in America.

His writing fuses personal narrative with cultural analysis, urging readers to confront inherited pain while imagining new possibilities for wholeness. Bill is the author of *This Is My New Foundation*, *Twins in the Mirror*, and *The Hidden Bruise*, each providing a distinct perspective on emotional resilience, identity, and restoration. His prose resonates with those who have been taught to endure rather than feel, and creates space for conversations once considered off-limits.

Bailey lives with his wife, Hazel, whose steadfast support anchors much of his healing. Together, they remain devoted to the power of stories to mend, renew, and reimagine what is possible for future generations.

Acknowledgments

To my wife, Hazel

Your love has anchored and sheltered me, constant through highs, storms, and silence. You never gave up, standing by me when I couldn't stand by myself. Your patience, strength, and quiet faith have shown me that I am never alone. This healing foundation was possible because you held the pieces while I learned to rebuild. I love you deeply and endlessly.

To my children

You are my heart and the legacy I will always cherish. Watching you grow, rise, and live your truths has given my life purpose wordlessly. Though I haven't always been perfect, I've loved you completely. You've taught me grace, joy, and why the fight for better was worth it. I cherish each of you.

Table of Contents

Prologue

Before We Begin

Some wounds don't bleed. They settle in. They reveal themselves in how we talk, how we love, and how we protect ourselves from those closest to us. They live in our habits and our hush, in quiet corners of our homes, unnoticed. These bruises appear not on our skin but in our spirit. They are the ones we were taught not to name.

I wrote this book to tell the truth. Not just my truth, but the ones I heard whispered in kitchens after funerals, in midnight calls, in church pews. I wrote it for the child who learned to be quiet to keep the peace. For the father who never learned to say "I'm sorry." For the mother who carried everything and never fell apart. For men who equate strength with silence. For women exhausted from saving others while breaking inside.

This book is not a callout. It's an invitation to look within—an invitation to return to your truest self and to the heart of what matters.

You may see yourself here. You may recognize your family, your past, or your present. Some parts may sting; others may feel like overdue relief. My only request: read with an open

1

heart and a soft hand. Some stories here may be heavy, but all aim to move us toward healing and growth.

We cannot repair what we refuse to face. We cannot heal what we were never allowed to feel. This is a book about feeling.

Before we begin, take a breath. Bring your story. There's room for it here.

CHAPTER 1

WHEN THE HURT COMES HOME

Chapter 1

When the Hurt Comes Home

Some houses are haunted—not by ghosts, but by grief. Not the kind of grief that cries out loud or slams doors in rage. This kind of lingers in the air, silent and heavy, like humidity before a storm. It clings to curtains, settles into furniture, and seeps into walls. This is the grief of what went unsaid, what was swallowed instead of spoken, what was endured with a tight jaw and lowered eyes. Many of us grew up in these homes. Love and pain lived side by side. Discipline blurred with fear. Silence was its own kind of language.

In my own childhood home, there was no grand tragedy to name. No headlines. No police report. The pain was more subtle, more insidious. It showed up in tone and tension. In long silences that followed short tempers. In the way we all moved around certain topics like they were furniture we'd learned not to bump into. There were rules no one had to say out loud: don't ask questions when Daddy's pacing. Don't show too much emotion. Don't cry in public. Pain wasn't denied. It was simply never acknowledged. That was how we survived. Survival, rather than healing, was the primary goal.

Children learn quickly which parts of themselves are welcome and which must be hidden. I learned to hide softness, swallow confusion, and replace questions with obedience. My mother loved me deeply, but I could see the weight she carried in her posture and eyes. She worked to hold everything together, and we pretended she was fine. No one taught her what to do with pain, so she carried it quietly and passed on silence to us.

Now, looking back, I see that trauma doesn't always arrive with a bang. Sometimes it comes like a slow leak. It lives in the unsaid, the unfinished, the unresolved. It hides behind Sunday clothes and prayer hands. It makes itself at home in routines— who speaks at the table, who doesn't, who gets hugged, who gets blamed, who disappears into themselves without anyone noticing. We often mistake these things for personality quirks or cultural norms, but they are often bruises wearing masks. We carry the legacy of those bruises into adulthood, into our relationships, into our own parenting, and call them normal because they've always been there.

My uncle once said, "We love hard in this family, but we don't talk much." I learned early on that love in our house wasn't quiet or distant—it was fierce, loyal, and loud when it needed to be. We would go to war for each other without hesitation. If someone outside the family came for one of us, the rest would show up—no questions, no doubt. That was never in question. But when the battle was internal, when the wounds were invisible, when the hurt came from within the family, that same love didn't know what to do with itself. We weren't taught to hold each other gently. We were taught to hold each other up. And sometimes, that meant ignoring what was breaking.

I've thought about this way of life for years—how it shaped me, how it shaped us. What my uncle meant, I now believe, is that we knew how to endure. We provided—money, food, advice, protection—but not emotional presence. We didn't know how to sit with pain without fixing or minimizing it. Vulnerability felt risky, so we armored up. We buried what we felt under work, jokes, prayer, and pride.

We became experts at keeping secrets—first from others, then ourselves. We convinced ourselves we were okay, that what we carried was normal. In that silence, something hardened—a kind of emotional callus. Not because we didn't feel, but because feeling had no place to go. So, we kept moving, smiling, surviving, and passed that silence down like an heirloom. We didn't mean to—but unspoken pain becomes tradition.

Some people inherit land. Some inherit recipes, debt, or family businesses. Others, like me, inherit silence. And silence is not empty. It is full of memories, of longings, of fears we didn't have the words for. We carried it the best we could. We laughed out loud at the holidays. Kept busy. Worked hard. Excelled. Still, the hurt found its way in. It showed up in anxiety we couldn't name, angry outbursts that surprised us, our inability to let others truly see us. The trauma didn't need to be dramatic to be real. It just had to be ours.

With this understanding, I've thought about this way of life for years—how it shaped me, how it shaped us. What my uncle meant, I now believe, is that we knew how to endure. We knew how to be strong, how to make sacrifices, and how to keep going. We knew how to provide—money, food, advice, protection—but not how to be emotionally present. We didn't know how to sit with each other's pain without trying to fix it or minimize it. Vulnerability felt foreign, even dangerous. Saying "I'm hurting" was too close to weakness. Saying "I need" was risky, as if it might be used against you later. So, we didn't say it. We armored up. We buried what we felt under work, under jokes, under prayer, under pride.

If you grew up in a home where love came with unspoken terms, where emotions were dangerous or inconvenient, where your sensitivity made you "too much"—you are not alone. If you've ever wondered why certain rooms or seasons or songs trigger something unexplainable in you, this may be why. If you've struggled to feel safe in places that are supposed to be safe, struggled to name your needs without guilt, struggled to believe that love doesn't have to hurt, you're in the right place.

With this context in mind, this chapter isn't about placing blame. It's about recognizing patterns. It's about naming what has been hidden, not to indict those who raised us, but to finally give ourselves permission to feel what we weren't allowed to before. It is about looking with tenderness at the younger versions of ourselves—the ones who were too afraid to speak, too loyal to question, too confused to understand what was happening. It's about realizing that some of the pain we carry didn't start with us, but it lives with us now, and it shapes more of our story than we realize.

To move forward, we must start at the beginning. We begin this book where many stories of pain do: at home. Not the home we presented to others, but the one we lived in when the curtains were drawn. The one where good people carried bad pain. Where children absorbed what was never explained. Where healing has yet to happen, because no one ever dared to say, "This hurt me."

CHAPTER 2

WHISPERS IN THE SANCTUARY

Chapter 2

Whispers in the Sanctuary

Not all sanctuaries—places we retreat for refuge—are sacred. Some are built with the best intentions and still become cages, trapping rather than protecting. Some are led by women who prayed for healing but never found it, who learned to manage pain by controlling the world around them. Women who confuse silence with order. Women who were never allowed to be soft demanded hardness from everyone in their care.

In our communities, sanctuaries are often more than just churches. They're spaces of supposed refuge: kitchens, living rooms, dinner tables on Sunday afternoons, bedrooms kept clean enough to make up for chaos no one dares to name. And often at the center of these sanctuaries is a woman—a mother, a grandmother, a godmother—whose love is undeniable, whose work is tireless, whose voice carries the power of law. She holds everything together. And still, sometimes, she also holds us in place, mixing safety with restraint.

We revere these women. We are here because of them. They survived things we can barely imagine. They endured men who disappeared, systems that discarded them, children who didn't listen, wounds that had no balm. And they did what they had to do: they got tough. They got loud. They got firm. They became both the foundation—steady base—and the fence—a barrier—of these sanctuaries. But somewhere in the building of these dual-purpose sanctuaries, a whisper crept in—a belief that to love a boy was to harden him, that to raise a man was to scrub him of softness.

The boys in these sanctuaries learned to be obedient, quiet, and grateful. We learned to clean the kitchen. We learned to speak when spoken to and never talk back. We learned how to present well. We learned to pray with our hands folded and our pain hidden. We were praised for being strong, polite, and composed. But no one asked what it cost us to become that way.

We weren't allowed to be unsure. We weren't allowed to be afraid. We couldn't say we didn't know who we were becoming. Vulnerability was dangerous. Sensitivity was punished. As we grew older and began to stumble—emotionally, spiritually, or relationally—the same women who had raised us didn't always know how to respond to our unraveling. They had taught us how to survive, not how to feel. They taught us how to provide, not how to process. They taught us how to carry the family name, but not how to carry our own wounds.

The truth is, they were doing what they had been taught to do. Many had been told from birth that the world wouldn't give them anything freely. So, they raised children they hoped would be unbreakable. They knew the danger of raising a tender boy in a violent, indifferent world. However, in their efforts to keep us safe, they overlooked the need to create space for our inner lives. The world was already threatening to kill us. Home should not have silenced us, too.

There were whispered rules in the sanctuary. Don't act soft. Don't talk back. Don't embarrass this family. These phrases were passed down like hymns. Beneath them were deeper, quieter messages. Don't cry where anyone can see you. Don't ask questions no one wants to answer. You will never need more than what we gave you. Those whispers echoed through generations. They were often delivered with love but rooted in fear.

I've sat across from men who couldn't name their pain until they were in their thirties. Some couldn't apologize without sounding like they were conceding a war. Some believed affection made them weak. Some didn't know how to hold a woman's feelings without feeling accused. Many were raised in sanctuaries and never learned to speak their own emotional language.

When we finally speak—when we begin to unlearn what silence taught us—it can feel like betrayal. It can feel like disloyalty. To critique the sanctuary feels like critiquing the woman who built it. But we must learn to separate honoring from romanticizing. Our mothers deserve gratitude. And truth. They deserve to be seen for their sacrifices, and for the harm they didn't mean to cause. They were powerful. They were exhausted. They did the best they could. Sometimes, it still wasn't enough.

This chapter isn't an indictment. It's a reckoning. It's an acknowledgment that sometimes the sanctuary—a space that should offer emotional safety—became instead a place where vulnerability was unsafe. Sometimes, the people who loved us most didn't give us what we most needed: emotional safety, space to be vulnerable, and freedom to cry without being punished for it. And now, we have to decide: will we continue building these kinds of sanctuaries, both shelters and cages? Or will we tear down the walls that silence, shame, and harden us before we're even fully formed?

We are not here to blame our mothers. Instead, we are here to unlearn what no longer serves us, honoring their legacy while seeking healing for ourselves.

We are here to whisper new things in the sanctuary. Things like "I'm scared." "I don't know how." "I love you." "I need help."

"I feel broken." We are here to speak what was once unspeakable. The boys coming after us shouldn't have to armor up just to eat dinner. They should grow up in spaces that feel like home, not performance halls where only the strong survive.

Because if healing doesn't happen in the sanctuary—our chosen place of refuge and sometimes restraint—it won't happen anywhere.

CHAPTER 3

PUBLIC FACES, PRIVATE FIGHTS

Chapter 3

Public Faces, Private Fights

"He was never taught to be a man—just to be a provider, a protector, and sometimes a problem."

They arrived at church in elegant attire. Their hats stretched like wings of quiet resistance; skirts pressed sharp as sermons; purses filled with peppermints, tissues, and unspoken prayers. Who were these women? The aunties, mamas, church mothers, and godmothers whose presence commanded reverence without raising their voices. You could smell the oil on their skin, feel the fire behind their eyes. They knew how to comfort and correct in the same breath—wisdom in motion. Yet behind those strong, sacred faces, there lingered a contradiction, too heavy to carry alone and too taboo to say out loud.

These women gave advice to the boys in their orbit, quoting scripture and spouting strength like inheritance. Yet, for many, they had never seen a boy grow into a whole man—not in their homes, and not in their husbands. They had raised sons into dependence, not maturity: boys who could build a barbecue pit but not a relationship; boys who could protect siblings from bullies but couldn't protect partners from emotional neglect;

boys present at family funerals but absent from their own inner lives. The truth is, many of these boys became men who never stopped needing their mothers to survive. They knew how to be loud, how to defend, how to disappear when they didn't have the right words. But they never learned to grieve. Never learned to say "I'm scared" without folding it into anger. Never learned to love without demanding to be rescued in return.

And the women—Lord, the women—kept showing up for them. Out of love, yes, but also out of fear. Out of guilt. Out of an unspoken belief that a mother's worth was tied to her ability to absorb everything: the failure, the fallout, the unmet expectations. These women paid bills, bailed sons out, whispered prayers over grown men sleeping on couches, and convinced themselves that loving harder might finally raise the man who'd never had a blueprint.

But here's the quiet heartbreak: You cannot mother a grown man into fatherhood. You cannot carry him across the threshold of his own responsibility. You cannot keep giving until he decides to give something back—to himself, to his children, to the world.

Your godfather had to learn this the hard way. No one gave him a manual. No one taught him how to balance his rage with reason, how to hold his family without falling apart himself. He had to piece it together from scraps—moments of clarity between chaos, hard lessons learned in courtrooms and kitchens, painful silences with sons who mirrored his own emotional ghosts. He became a father by first admitting that he had no idea how to be one. He raised himself into manhood because the one meant to teach him disappeared before the lesson began.

Still, the women wore their public faces—polished, poised, practiced. They smiled in church, ran the household, and held the family together, grace unacknowledged. Yet, behind closed doors, they unraveled quietly, tenderly, fiercely, fighting private battles with disappointment, emotional exhaustion, and the unspoken resentment of having to do it all over again—not for toddlers or teenagers, but for grown sons who never fully stepped into manhood.

They never got to be soft. Never got to break. Never got to say, "I'm tired of being strong." Because always, one more man-child needed saving. One more crisis to manage. One more son who mistook her survival instinct for a permanent safety net. And in the very spaces meant for refuge—church, home, even their own bedrooms—there was no room for the truth: "He should've learned this by now."

They never said, "I raised you once. And if I knew then what I know now, I might have done things differently. I'll walk beside you; I'll guide you, but I cannot raise you again." [bell hooks, The Will to Change]

In the daily weight of covering for men unequipped to cover others. In the quiet grief of watching your son become the kind of man you tried to protect him from. In the guilt, wondering if your love made him emotionally helpless, or your exhaustion made him emotionally absent. In the fear that he will raise children the same way he was raised: halfway whole, emotionally guarded, spiritually hungry.

This is not about blame. This is about sorrow. This is about the kind of wound that doesn't bleed but still causes deep bruising. The public face says, "Everything's fine." The private fight says, "I'm holding this family together with my bare hands."

It's time we stop expecting women to carry that alone. It's time we tell the truth about the boys who were never taught how to become men. And it's time we stop confusing survival with manhood. Because a man who's only been taught to protect will eventually turn his protection into control. A man who's only been taught to provide will measure his worth in money and miss the emotional poverty in his home. And a man who's been taught that he is a problem will either spend his life apologizing for existing, or defending himself even when no one is attacking.

We owe ourselves a better blueprint.

And we owe our women a place to put the burden down.

CHAPTER 4

FEAR
IN THE
BLOODLINE

Chapter 4

Fear in the Bloodline

"The first language we learned wasn't always love. Sometimes it was fear disguised as discipline; silence dressed as strength."

We were raised not just by people, but by their wounds.

By their caution. By the prayers whispered into pillows and the rage swallowed at dinner. *Don't talk back. Don't cry. Don't let them see you weak.* These weren't just house rules. They were survival codes passed down like heirlooms, shaped by slavery, segregation, and silence. We weren't born afraid. We were taught.

"Boy, stop crying before I give you something to cry about," my mother snapped—loud enough for everyone to hear.

It was my birthday. I don't remember what made me cry—maybe the wrong gift, maybe a heavy feeling I couldn't name—but I remember her voice cutting through the music and laughter like a slap in the air.

I froze, cheeks wet, my breath caught, and fists shaking. My mother loomed above, her jaw hard, arms crossed, eyes daring me to continue. I looked up, my heart raw—not just hurt, but stripped and shamed.

The grown men around us didn't flinch. Nobody looked my way. They just turned the ribs on the grill like nothing had happened. Like they hadn't just watched a boy learn—publicly—that softness was dangerous. That emotion made you a target. That manhood came early, whether you were ready or not.

That was the moment I started holding things in.

But that's what fear does when it wears a familiar face—it hides in plain sight.

My own father was a ghost. His presence meant absence. A voice through court documents or rare phone calls, not hallway steps or 'I'm proud of you' moments. His silence taught me more than disappointment—it taught me how to disappear, how to pretend I needed nothing, how to armor up with those who were supposed to love me. If love left too, maybe it was safer not to ask for it at all.

And then—one day—he appeared.

He came to my high school graduation with a suit on, five hundred dollars in his pocket, and a promise on his lips:

"You don't have to worry about college. I got you."

For a moment, I wanted to believe that maybe this was how the story would turn out. That maybe this man—who hadn't been there for my childhood—could somehow be there for my future.

But I had lived too much already. The boy in me had grown up the hard way.

So I looked him in the eye and said,

"I'm a man now. I made it all these years without you. I know your sister, but I don't know you. And I've come this far on my own. I'll keep going."

He left.

And I never saw him again.

That moment didn't just mark a turning point in my relationship with him—it revealed something about the inheritance of fear and absence. You see, he thought showing up with money and pride could fix years of distance and silence. He believed that manhood was about *arrival*, but I had already learned it was about *endurance*.

He didn't understand. I had already raised myself.

So many of us are forced to raise ourselves in the shadow of men who never learned to be fathers. Men who return briefly, hoping pride will cover up the wounds their absence created. But pride isn't parenting. A promise at the finish line doesn't erase who missed the start.

His absence shaped me, but not in the way he may have imagined. It taught me to stand up on my own. It taught me that manhood is not what you inherit by blood, but what you earn by showing up—again and again, especially when it's hard, when it's quiet, when no one's watching.

That day, I wasn't rejecting a father. I was claiming my foundation.

One built from truth. From scars. From survival.

And yes, from fear. But not the kind that keeps you bound. The kind you stare down and walk through anyway.

The Fathers Who Stayed… But Still Didn't Show Up

Some fathers didn't leave the house.

They sat on the couch, beer in hand, TV flashing like a second life. They were there at dinner, there when the door opened—but never *really* there. They didn't ask about your day, your friends, or your dreams. Their presence was a shadow over the room, never wrapping around you.

They didn't teach their sons how to be men—they just taught them how to endure one.

I've seen boys grow up in houses with fathers who never said their names with affection. Boys who watched their daddies drink through Sunday afternoons, yelling at the screen, never once looking over to say, *"I'm proud of you."*

They grew up in the same book I was written into—pages full of longing and unfinished sentences. Like me, they pieced together manhood from scraps: overheard conversations, unspoken pain, the ache of not being seen by their father.

A father's brokenness—absent or seated close—teaches a boy to shrink, to numb, to hide his true heart. Sometimes the scariest silence is the kind that seeps into you day after day, right beside you, growing heavier each hour.

Because the father who stays but never speaks, never touches, never listens, creates a different kind of bruise: one that tells the child, *you're not worth the effort.*

And so, we carry that.

We carry that into our relationships, our parenting, our silences. We either repeat the wound or break the cycle—but only if we name it.

Only if we stop saying, *"At least he was there,"* and start asking, *"But did he show up?"*

Breaking the Bloodline Contract

This isn't about blame. It's about mapping our emotional inheritance. The places where fear was planted, watered, and left to grow wild.

We grew up where the belt set boundaries, and silence meant respect. Boys weren't allowed fear, girls learned to stay small for safety. Prayer was the only therapy—even God grew tired if your voice cracked too often. Love was there, buried in casseroles, folded into laundry, tucked behind rent payments and school forms. But fear was louder. Fear got to us first.

It taught us how to flinch before we spoke. How to read the room before we dared enter it fully. How to protect ourselves from people who were supposed to be our protectors.

"I only did what I knew," my aunt once whispered during a late-night talk. "Mama beat me with a switch till my legs bled. So, when I only used my hand on my boys, I thought I was doing better."

She looked down, her fingers twisting in her lap.

"But I still see it in their eyes," she said. "That fear. That shame. That silence."

So, we carry it. This bloodline fear. Sometimes with defiance. Sometimes with denial. Sometimes with tears that only fall behind closed doors.

But here's the thing: **inheritance doesn't mean inevitability**.

What was passed down can be laid down. We can break the rules that broke us. We can name the things our parents couldn't. We can love our children into softness without fearing that the world will harden them.

Because fear may have gotten to us first—
But it doesn't have to be the last voice they hear. We get to decide what echoes after us. We get to end with love.

CHAPTER 5

BLACK BOYS, BROKEN FATHERS

Chapter 5

Black Boys, Broken Fathers

Some of us were raised by men who had never been fathered themselves. There may have been a man in the house, but he wasn't a father—just a figure holding space. We learned manhood through absence, and silence was the first language we spoke fluently.

There's a quiet hunger in a Black boy with no father—a steady ache for footsteps that never come, a longing for warmth he's never felt. He swallows his wishes, pretending not to care, while every part of him aches for a voice that finally tells him he matters.

Some fathers were gone before we could walk; others stayed long enough to leave damage. No matter if they vanished or numbed themselves with alcohol, anger, or distance, the result was the same: boys grew into men, still looking for someone to affirm them, correct them, love them without condition.

I remember a cousin of mine, no older than eight, holding a plastic bat in the front yard like it was a sword.
"You gonna play with me, Uncle?" he asked one of the older men at the barbecue.
"Nah," the man mumbled, barely glancing up from his beer.
"Go find somebody your size."

The boy's face cracked for a split second—pain running across it like a shadow—but he forced a smile, like he was used to hiding disappointment. Like he'd already practiced wanting less, needing less.

That's the training no one talks about—those early lessons Black boys receive about being too needy, too emotional, too open. We learn to close ourselves off before the world has the chance to slam the door, becoming fluent in silence because we think that's strength.

But beneath it all, what we really are is quietly, deeply hurt.

Many of our fathers were never taught how to love. They were taught how to provide, how to discipline, how to survive—but not how to sit with their children and be *seen* by them. As a result, we got rules without relationship, presence without intimacy. And for some of us, we got nothing at all.

And that *nothing* shaped us.

We became men who confused anger with authority. Men who raised their voices before we learned to raise our children. Men who stood at altars and promised loyalty, but couldn't share our emotions without feeling exposed.

Because no one ever taught us how.

My friend once told me that his father worked two jobs and spent his evenings on the porch, beer in hand, his eyes fixed on the darkness as if it owed him something. And whatever time he had left, he gave to the card table, not his children. "He never beat me," he said. "But he never *saw* me either."

That was the wound—his father didn't leave, but he didn't show up either. So, my friend spent his adult life trying to be everything his father wasn't… until he burned out trying.

We inherit the wounds of our fathers, not always through their actions, but through their absence.

And we pass those wounds down—sometimes wrapped in discipline, sometimes masked as protection, sometimes disguised as ambition. Beneath it all remains a boy still waiting to be chosen.

The Apprenticeship We Never Gained

Some of us thought that becoming fathers ourselves would fix what was broken, believing that if we just showed up, we'd be different. Better.

And maybe we were. Still, showing up isn't the same as being *available*.

You can be in the room and still feel like a stranger. You can bring home a paycheck and still offer no comfort. You can provide everything except the one thing your child needs most—*you*.

Being available requires more than presence.

It requires healing. Intention. Emotional literacy.
A willingness to feel what our fathers never dared touch.

The truth is:

We never had the apprenticeship of fatherhood.

We were never shown how to hold our child when they're afraid. Never taught how to say *"I'm proud of you"* without choking on the emotion. Never told that discipline without relationship breeds rebellion—and that love without tenderness feels like absence.

How could we learn?

You can't apprentice under a man who never went to
fatherhood school.
You can't learn how to build a bridge from someone who
only ever knew how to burn one down.

So, we made it up as we went along.
We stumbled through diapers, tantrums, and teenage silences.
We overcorrected or underinvested.
We parented through trial and error. Through pain and hope.

And some of us—despite all odds—are getting it right. Or at least, better.

Yet even the best of us finds that ache lingering—a quiet longing that refuses to fade.
That longing for the elder who would've shown us how.
The father who would've said, *"Watch me. Walk with me. Let me teach you how to love without fear."*

We didn't get that.

Now, it's up to us to become what we never received.
To be the blueprint we were never handed.
So now, it's on us to become what we never received, to father with intention instead of imitation.
To raise children who don't have to recover from their upbringing.

This is our responsibility now: to give our children the apprenticeship in fatherhood we never experienced ourselves. By intentionally guiding, affirming, and loving them, we become the blueprint for emotional availability, breaking the cycle for the next generation.

CHAPTER 6

THE WOMEN WHO HAD TO SWALLOW FIRE

Chapter 6

The Women Who Had to Swallow Fire

"They held the heat in their throats. Carried it in their backs. And smiled like it never burned."

Women Who Endured Pain Silently

To "swallow fire" is to carry rage, grief, disappointment, and exhaustion in your chest—and say nothing. Not because you want to. Because *you have to.* Because saying something might break everything. Because silence is safer than truth in a world that won't hold your pain gently.

These were the women who:

- Endured emotional or physical abuse in silence.
- Carried the weight of families while being undervalued.
- Bit their tongues to keep peace in homes that weren't peaceful.
- Buried their dreams to raise children, survive men, and hold communities together.

Swallowing fire means *taking in what should have burned everything down—and surviving it anyway.*

Women Who Were Forced to Be Strong All the Time

This is the story of **Black women** in particular—those taught to be *invincible by default.* They weren't asked if they could handle it. No one asked. They were simply expected to.

Their fire wasn't just pain. It was:

- The pressure to never break down.
- The anger they had to suppress to be called "ladylike."
- The injustice they endured quietly so they wouldn't be labeled "difficult."
- The tears they cried in the shower after telling everybody else, *"I got it."*

Swallowing fire meant absorbing every flame—every insult, every betrayal, every breakdown—and still showing up. Still cooking. Still leading. Still loving. Still praying.
Even when they were burned out from the inside.

The Invisible Labor of Black Womanhood

The women in this chapter didn't just carry pain—they carried **entire generations.**

- They raised children alone while covering for absent men.

- They disciplined their sons and daughters not out of cruelty, but out of fear—because they knew the world wouldn't give their children grace.
- They swallowed their own healing so their families wouldn't unravel.

They didn't just hold the fire—they swallowed it whole so the people they loved could keep breathing.

Fire as Truth They Couldn't Speak

There were truths these women never said out loud. There wasn't room. There wasn't safety. There wasn't permission.

So, they buried those truths in casseroles, beneath their church hats, and between the lines of whispered prayers. These women weren't just mothers—they were also full-time workers. Since the 1960s, Black women—more than any other ethnic group—have had to live as two people in one body: provider and nurturer, breadwinner and backbone, holding up households with strength that was expected, but rarely supported.

They swallowed truths like:

- *"I'm tired."*
- *"This marriage is killing me."*

- *"I deserve more."*
- *"I wish I could've left."*

They held back so their children wouldn't have to.

But the fire didn't go away.

It smoldered beneath their strength. It shaped their shadows.

It burned behind their eyes and beneath their smiles.

And Still, They Showed Up

Evelyn

Evelyn swallowed fire.

She endured emotional and physical abuse and never told a soul—not a neighbor, not a brother, not even herself in the mirror. She knew how to smile through pain. She knew how to walk into church with her hair pressed and her heels polished. Even when her spirit was bruised. Even when she was barely holding on.

She carried secrets like scripture—quietly, faithfully, and without question.

You could smell the starch in her clothes before you noticed the weariness in her eyes. And if you asked her how she was doing, she'd say, *"Blessed."*

But she wasn't. She was breaking. Slowly. Silently.

Still, she cooked, prayed, attended family reunions, wrote

birthday cards, and never let the fire in her chest burn the house down.

That was her sacrifice. And her silence.

Lorraine

Lorraine carried the fire.
She bore the weight of everyone's needs—her own last. She raised kids who weren't hers. She fed husbands who didn't stay. She stretched every dollar as if it were scripture.

Lorraine never sat down. Her life was a series of errands, favors, and unfinished sentences. She didn't need to be told she was strong—she was reminded of it every time someone expected her to carry just one more thing.

They didn't thank her.
They didn't ask if she needed help.
They just called Lorraine.

She was the backbone and the afterthought all at once.

But beneath her busy hands was a tired heart. One who longed for someone to say, *"You can rest now."*
But rest never came. So, she kept going, swallowing, and carrying.

Miriam

Miriam bit her tongue until it bled.

She knew how to keep peace in a house that hadn't known peace in years. She said *yes* when she wanted to scream *no*. She stayed. Every part of her spirit was whispering: *run*.

Miriam was loyal to the children, to the church, to the image of a family that looked whole from the outside.

She didn't speak back because she'd been taught that women who talked too much lost everything.
So she stayed quiet. Smiled at dinner. Folded towels with precision. And cried in the bathroom while the water ran, so no one would hear.

Her silence was not weakness—it was strategy. It was survival.

And though no one gave her a medal, she carried generations on the strength of her silence.

Delores

Delores was fired, but she was told to put it out.

She had a voice like thunder. A mind that moved too fast for some. A heart that wanted more than what tradition allowed. But she learned early that fire made people uncomfortable.

So she made herself smaller. Straighter. Quieter.

She tucked in her ambition, clipped her curiosity, and cut her opinions into bite-sized pieces.

She smiled at men who dismissed her. She bit her tongue in rooms where she was overqualified to speak. She stood behind pulpits and podiums and wondered if she'd ever be allowed to *show up fully*.

Delores didn't just swallow fire—she buried it. And still, she led, taught, and kept showing up for everyone— even when no one showed up for her.

The Burn Beneath the Silence

They swallowed the fire so no one else had to burn.

They held in screams, sorrow, fury, and grief. They carried the weight of families, faith, fragile men, and complicated legacies. They kept things whole that were already breaking. The world called them *strong* and rarely asked if they were okay.

They endured because there was no clear path to escape. Because leaving would've meant losing everything. Because telling the truth would've cracked the image too wide open.

Because survival for a Black woman has always come at the cost of softness.

But here's what we now understand:

That kind of strength has a cost.

It costs you your breath. Your voice. Your body. Your joy.
It buries your laughter under duty. It teaches your daughters
to suffer quietly. It tells your sons that love is labor, not
presence. Not touch. Not softness.
And it builds a legacy of silence that spans generations.

Evelyn. Lorraine. Miriam. Delores.
They all did what they had to do.

But what they were forced to carry in silence—**we must now
name aloud.**

We must make room for their pain.
Not just their endurance, not just their utility, not just their
reputation.

Their *pain*.

We must say: *You should've been able to rest.*
You should've been allowed to scream.
You should've had the space to say, "This is too much,"
without being punished for it.

Because healing begins when the fire isn't swallowed—
But finally spoken.

And if we are to build something better, we must begin by telling the truth:

They survived. But they deserved more than survival.
They deserved softness.
They deserved safety.
They deserved to live fully, not just hold everything together.

And we owe it to them to say:

Never again will silence be the price of strength.

CHAPTER 7

WHAT THE PAIN TAUGHT US

Chapter 7

What the Pain Taught Us

"The wound is where the light enters—but only if we're willing to look."

We've named the bruises. We remember the fathers who never came home, the mothers who swallowed fire to keep the peace, and the children who grew up learning silence as their first language. We've traced pain across generations like a family heirloom—handled carefully, passed down quietly, and never fully unpacked. And now we're standing in the middle of the truth, asking the only question that matters next: What have we learned—and how do we begin to fix what's been broken?

The pain taught us that silence isn't safety. It showed us that keeping secrets to preserve the family name only keeps the family in a cycle of deception. We learned that swallowing truth doesn't heal—it hides. And what we hide, we pass on. We've seen how unspoken grief can become a policy in a household. How silence masquerades as strength, and how endurance becomes the enemy of softness. We've mistaken control for care, absence for independence, and emotional distance for discipline. And in doing so, we've raised children who grow up whole in body but fractured in spirit.

We've also learned that presence alone is not enough. Being in the room doesn't mean you've shown up. Paying bills doesn't mean you've paid attention. A father can sit at the table and still leave his child starving for affection. A mother can cook every meal and still be too exhausted to see her child's pain. This is what the pain taught us—that love requires more than survival. It demands presence, truth, softness, and repair.

So, how do we begin to fix the situation?

We start by telling the truth—saying what happened, admitting what we did. We stop hiding behind tradition and embrace accountability. We apologize as a practice of healing, not a performance. We listen without interrupting and hold space without defending. We stop using "that's just how I was raised" to excuse damage. Survival is no longer the goal—healing is.

We go to therapy. We stop laughing off trauma and turning wounds into personality or culture. We learn to love again, or maybe for the first time. We teach children that strength is not silence and softness isn't weakness. We parent differently, hug longer, listen more, and sit still with our pain instead of passing it on.

We stop romanticizing struggle. Our mothers deserved more than resilience. Our fathers deserved more than pressure. Our children deserve more than protection. They deserve joy. They deserve parents who are emotionally present, who speak life instead of fear, who offer love that doesn't come with conditions.

The pain taught us that healing will never come through pretending. It will never arrive if we continue to avoid what broke us. The healing begins the moment we stop performing and start practicing truth. It begins when we stop saying, *"That's just how I am,"* and start asking, *"Who do I want to become?"* It begins when we choose to feel. When we choose to stay. When we choose to name the bruise, not just cover it.

We can't fix everything overnight. But we can stop the bleeding. We can change the direction. We can tell the truth in our families and build new traditions rooted in presence, softness, and care. What the pain taught us is that we are not alone. That we are not beyond repair. That we can be the ones to end the silence. To say, *"This ends with me."* And to mean it.

The lesson is not just in what happened, but in what we allowed, what we ignored, and what we passed down without knowing. We've learned that pain doesn't disappear just because you don't speak it. We've learned that silence breeds confusion, that children grow up filling in emotional blanks with their own shame. We've learned that being a provider doesn't make you present. That being strong doesn't mean you're whole. We've learned that love requires more than duty—it requires vulnerability, accountability, and the capacity for repair. And if we could do it all again, we would listen more and lecture less. We would ask our children what they needed before telling them who to become. We would say "I'm sorry" sooner. We would stop protecting the image and start protecting the spirit. We would stop using toughness as a substitute for love and learn how to sit beside pain without trying to fix it first. What we could have done better is simple, but not easy: we could have loved without fear. We could have broken the silence sooner. We could have told the truth. But now that we know better, we will.

CHAPTER 8

REPAIR REQUIRES TRUTH

Chapter 8

Repair Requires Truth

"You cannot heal what you refuse to name. You cannot repair what you pretend never broke."

Healing is not a vibe. It's not a slogan. Not a sermon. Not a weekend retreat. Real healing—deep, generational, gut-wrenching healing—requires something most families avoid: the truth. Not the version we tell to save face. Not the version we shrink to keep the peace. The real, whole, unvarnished truth. The kind that stings when it's first spoken. The kind that pulls the scabs off the stories we've been trying to forget.

You cannot build a new foundation on a lie or move forward while dragging silence. Some seek reconciliation without reckoning, forgiveness without confession, peace without admitting harm.

But repair begins with truth. And the truth is not always gentle.

Families have a way of burying what breaks them. People come to holidays and pass around sweet potatoes, pretending like nothing ever happened. A child gets whipped for something they didn't do, and no one ever says sorry. A father disappears for five years and returns with a gift and a grin, and everyone is supposed to be grateful. A mother yells too much, loves too little, and one day just says, *"You know I did the best I could."*

But "the best I could" doesn't repair a wounded child. It can't. "The best I could" doesn't explain why love felt like punishment. Or why silence was louder than any scream. The truth is, intentions don't erase impact. Healing doesn't come from avoidance. It comes from telling the truth and telling it in full.

If a child grew up thinking everything was their fault because no adult ever took responsibility, that is a bruise that deserves naming. If a partner learned to mistrust love because the people who claimed to love them also controlled them, that is a wound that cannot be erased with good behavior now. It has to be met with *truth*—spoken, held, and owned.

Repair isn't about blame. It's about *accountability*. It's about someone saying, *"Yes, that happened. And I hurt you. And I will not hide behind excuses anymore."*

It's about going back for the child in you who didn't understand. About facing the version of yourself that stayed quiet when you should have spoken. Naming who you became because of what you were never given. That's where the work begins. That's where healing starts—not in pretending you're okay, but in admitting what you survived to get here.

Repair requires an apology. But not just *"I'm sorry you feel that way."* That's not the truth—that's manipulation in a nice suit. Real apology says, *"I see what I did. I understand how it shaped you. And I will not do it again."* It says, *"I failed you, and I'm here to own it."*

Repair also means listening—really listening. It means letting someone else have the microphone, even if what they say convicts you. It means not interrupting with your shame. It means not rushing to defend your version of the story when someone is still struggling to tell theirs.

It also means repairing yourself, telling the truth to the mirror. Saying out loud, *"That wasn't normal. I deserved better. That pain shaped me."*

Because what we don't repair, we repeat.

And repeating the wound is how we lose the future while holding onto the past. But telling the truth? That's how we make space for something new. For peace that's not built on silence. For relationships that are safe, not just tolerable. For generations that won't have to grow up swallowing the pain we refused to name.

So, let's stop shrinking the truth to protect people's feelings. Let's refuse to pretend the damage didn't matter. Let's reject "let's just move on." If the foundation is cracked, we cannot build on top of it until it is repaired. Start by telling the truth—even if it's late, even if it's uncomfortable, even if your voice shakes.

Because the only thing more painful than the truth is living your whole life pretending it didn't happen.

But repair cannot stop at the front door of our homes. **We need help.** Not only to help us understand our pain, but also to help create a society that doesn't keep recreating it.

We need schools that don't criminalize Black boys for emotions they weren't taught to manage. Teachers must understand trauma doesn't always look like a bruise—it can be silence, fidgeting, "disobedience," or a child wanting to be alone. Our neighborhoods need mental health resources, not just police. We need policies that fund prevention, not punishment, and churches that preach accountability *and* offer therapy. Communities should make it safe to feel, not just perform strength.

We need help reshaping local and national government, not just to fix potholes or balance budgets, but to build *systems of care, reparative justice*, and *emotional equity*. We need leaders who understand that healing isn't just personal—it's political. That unhealed communities become unstable communities. That cycles of harm don't break because one family does better—they break when *society steps in to support that family doing better.*

Because it's not enough to tell people to "do the work" if the systems they live in are still punishing them for being broken.

Yes, we must tell the truth. But now it's time to demand a society willing to *hear* that truth—and change because of it. Let's not just hope for transformation. Let's push for it.

We need truth commissions in our schools. We need listening sessions in our city halls. We need leaders who aren't afraid to say, *"The people have been hurting, and we have failed them."*

If repair is going to be genuine, it must be rooted in the *relationship* between people and power.

We can't afford to keep placing the burden of healing solely on the shoulders of individuals. We need institutions that don't just apologize—but restructure. We need truth in the streets and in the legislature. We need policies that reflect the pain we've uncovered—and invest in futures that don't repeat it.

Because repair isn't just personal—it's cultural. It's communal. It's political.

And it begins with us. Speak the truth—today. Choose truth, choose repair, and make it real.

CHAPTER 9

GRACE IS NOT AMNESIA

Chapter 9

Grace Is Not Amnesia

"To forgive is not to forget. To heal is not to pretend."

Grace is not pretending nothing happened. Grace is choosing to live fully, even though something did. Healing doesn't erase the past; it means facing what broke us, naming it, and daring to build something better. Grace isn't letting others off the hook—it's freeing yourself from shame and the belief that pain or mere survival is your inheritance.

Because we are not just what happened to us. We are what we choose to do with the truth.

We've looked back long enough. Now we turn forward—not forgetting, but *remembering with clarity*. Not erasing, but *rewriting*. Not just surviving, but becoming.

Personal Repair

We begin with the self. Grace means choosing to tell the truth about your own pain and its impact. You don't need to wait for permission to heal.

Action Steps:

- Begin therapy or community healing circles.

- Write the letter you were never brave enough to send—then decide whether to send it or simply release it.
- Tell your children the truth about your story so they don't inherit silence.

Family Repair

Healing starts where harm began. You don't need everyone to agree to heal, but you do need someone to take the first step.

Action Steps:

Host "truth dinners" where stories are told and not judged.

Create new rituals: instead of Sunday silence, make space for Sunday listening.

What if we replaced the drinks and the deck of cards with honest questions and the kind of listening we never got as kids?

Encourage intergenerational conversations—not just correction, but curiosity.

Community Repair

We need new institutions that don't just reflect old pain in prettier packaging.

Organizations We Need:

- Neighborhood Healing Centers – trauma-informed, culturally rooted, led by people who reflect the community.
- The Fatherhood School – a space where men gather to unlearn shame and learn to nurture.
- Mothers Who Swallowed Fire Coalition – support circles for women who carried too much alone.
- Youth Truth Labs – safe spaces in schools and churches where kids can name what's hurting before it hardens.

Action Steps:

- Fund therapists who look like us and speak our languages.
- Partner with barbershops, beauty salons, and faith centers to become hubs of emotional health.
- Train coaches and mentors to recognize trauma, rather than punishing it.

Policy & Structural Repair

Healing won't stick if the systems still punish our pain.

Blueprint for Systemic Change:

- Mental Health Equity Act: mandate free trauma-informed counseling in public schools and underserved neighborhoods.
- Justice Redesign Boards: Empower impacted community members to reshape juvenile justice and family court systems.
- Truth and Reconciliation Councils: Every city should establish a space to acknowledge the legacy of harm in housing, policing, education, and public health.

Action Steps:

- Advocate for restorative justice in schools and courts.
- Elect leaders who've lived what they legislate.
- Invest in prevention, not just punishment—housing, healing, childcare, and mental wellness.

Cultural Repair

We need art, stories, and media that reflect our complexity—not just our wounds.

Action Steps:

- Fund filmmakers, writers, and musicians telling the full truth—not just survival, but softness.

- Include healing in every social justice agenda: if the movement doesn't include mental health, it's incomplete.
- Shift the narrative from "strong Black woman" to *fully human Black woman*. From "absent Black father" to *healing Black man*.

The Tools Are Here—Now Let's Use Them to Heal

We've never had more power in our hands than we do right now. The internet, artificial intelligence (AI), and digital platforms, such as Zoom, Instagram, and specialized mental health apps, have changed everything. However, instead of merely entertaining or distracting us, these tools can be repurposed for repair, personal healing, community restoration, and structural change.

Digital Healing Spaces

- Online therapy networks such as Therapy for Black Girls and BetterHelp now make culturally competent care more accessible.
- Virtual support groups for Black fathers, mothers healing from trauma, or youth in crisis give people the safety to speak without shame.
- We can host digital healing circles using Zoom, Instagram Live, or private apps, facilitating truth-

telling conversations that would not have been possible in person before.

AI for Mental Health and Storytelling

- AI tools, such as guided journaling apps, storytelling bots, or reflective chatbots, can help individuals process trauma through journaling, storytelling, or guided reflection.
- It can help people write their own narratives—naming pain, reframing it, and releasing it.
- Therapists and healers can use AI platforms to create personalized wellness plans, coaching prompts, and learning tools more efficiently, leveraging apps like Woebot or Lyra.

Educate, Mobilize, Organize

- The internet enables us to share healing practices in real-time across generations and geographies.
- Young people use platforms like TikTok to destigmatize therapy. Elders share hard-earned wisdom in Facebook groups and YouTube videos.
- We can build digital organizations—such as fatherhood schools, maternal healing networks, and truth labs—that start in group chats on apps like WhatsApp or Slack and grow into movements.

Rebuild with Data and Voice

- AI and tech can help communities analyze racial disparities, trauma patterns, and system failures—turning stories into *evidence*.

- We can design policy using lived experience as the blueprint.

- AI platforms can help draft healing-centered curriculum, legislation, and justice reform models. We can reclaim the system—data-first, community-led, utilizing tools such as machine learning data dashboards and collaborative writing apps.

Podcast Concept: The Hidden Bruise Circle

Purpose:

A space where people can **share personal truths in 4 minutes,** and then **receive 4 minutes of healing,** reflective feedback from the group—no fixing, no judgment, just witnessing.

Proposed Format: 8 Minutes of Healing

1. **Segment One: "Tell the Bruise" (4 minutes)**
   - One person shares a personal story of pain, breakthrough, silence, or survival.
   - Stories can be anonymous, named, or read aloud by a narrator.
   - Each speaker gets 4 uninterrupted minutes.

2. **Segment Two: "Hold the Mirror" (4 minutes)**
   - A small group (2–3 listeners) responds—not with advice, but with reflections.
   - They say what resonated. What mirrored something in them. What truth did they hear?
   - It's a practice of emotional witnessing, not emotional correction.

Structure for Each Episode

- Intro (1–2 min): Brief theme ("Fathers We Missed", "The Fire She Swallowed", etc.)
- Main Story (4 min)
- Reflections (4 min)
- Closing prompt (1 min): "What's your bruise? What truth are you ready to name?"

Why This Works

- Short time = low pressure, high focus
- Built-in healing structure: speak, then be seen.
- Promotes community literacy: not just storytelling, but deep listening.
- Can be recorded in-person, over Zoom, or submitted as voice memos.

Optional Features:

- Include a rotating co-host who models emotional feedback.
- Weekly themes pulled from The Hidden Bruise chapters.
- Community call-ins or listener letters to feature at the end.

But the key is this: these tools must serve the people, not surveil them. They must be built with care, not control. And they must reflect the truth of our stories, not erase them.

Technology can't replace healing.
However, it can support, scale, and spread it—if we lead the way.

Final Reflection

Grace is not forgetting; it's remembering with eyes wide open.
It's living beyond your wound.
It's knowing the bruise didn't break you, and refusing to pass it down.

We are not waiting on saviors.
We are becoming sanctuaries.
In our homes. In our schools. In our stories.
In our systems. In our silence, once filled.
We are the repair.

This is the new foundation

Your Hidden Bruise

An invitation to reflect, name, and begin your own healing.

You've read the stories. You've felt the ache. You've remembered things that may have stayed buried for years. Now, it's your turn.

This page is for you, not to fix anything, but to name what has been hidden. Because healing begins with naming. And sometimes, writing is how we finally find the words.

Take a breath. Let honesty rise. These questions aren't here to pressure you. They're here to hold space.

Write, reflect, or just sit with these prompts:

What bruise have you carried that no one ever saw?

(Where does it live—in your silence, your relationships, your body?)

_____

_____

_____

What truth were you never allowed to speak growing up?

(What would happen if you spoke it now?)

_____

_____

_____

Who taught you to hide your pain?

(And what might you want to say to them today?)

_____

_____

_____

What did love look like in your home?

(Was it soft? Was it loud? Was it conditional?)

_____

_____

_____

Where did you learn that your feelings were too much?

(What does that child in you still need to hear?)

_____

_____

_____

What patterns are you ready to break?

(What silence will end with you?)

_____

_____

_____

What does healing look like—for you?

(Not for your family. Not for appearances. But for your heart.)

_____

_____

_____

This is your sanctuary now. There are no wrong answers. There is no shame here. Just space.

Your hidden bruise matters—because _you_ matter. And naming it may be the most radical act of healing you ever do.

www.ingramcontent.com/pod-product-compliance
Lightning Source LLC
Chambersburg PA
CBHW071239090426
42736CB00014B/3151